George Wharton James

Pasadena and the Mount Lowe Railway

The Ideal Health and Pleasure Resort of the World

George Wharton James

Pasadena and the Mount Lowe Railway
The Ideal Health and Pleasure Resort of the World

ISBN/EAN: 9783337067984

Printed in Europe, USA, Canada, Australia, Japan

Cover: Foto ©Andreas Hilbeck / pixelio.de

More available books at **www.hansebooks.com**

MOUNT LOWE RAILWAY.

THE IDEAL HEALTH AND PLEASURE RESORT OF THE WORLD.

BY G. WHARTON JAMES, F. R. A. S.

General Offices: Grand Opera House Block, Pasadena, Cal.
Los Angeles Office: Los Angeles Safe Deposit and Trust Co., Stimson Block, Corner Third and Spring Streets.

General View of PASADENA and the Mountains Climbed by the MOUNT LOWE RAILWAY. Photographed from the Tower of President Lowe's Residence.

PASADENA

AND THE

MOUNT LOWE RAILWAY.

....

INTRODUCTORY.

The praises of Pasadena have been sung in all tongues and in all lands, and her claims as a place of permanent residence, or as a winter and *summer* resort for tourists and invalids are generally and gracefully conceded. Hence it is not my intention in the following pages to make this a hand-book to Pasadena. I propose merely to speak in general terms of the advantages she offers to all who come within her boundaries, whether for a short time or permanently, and then to refer more specifically to those places in Pasadena which are connected through Professor Lowe with the Mount Lowe Railway. The railway itself is the chief motive of the pamphlet. Visitors desire to carry away a descriptive reminder of the scenes and wonders they have enjoyed, and residents often wish to send such an account to their Eastern friends.

After a short ramble around Pasadena, and a brief sketch of the career of Professor T. S. C. Lowe, to whom the world owes the Mount Lowe Railway, the remaining part of the pamphlet is devoted to a description of the scenes witnessed in riding over this railway from Altadena to the highest summits of the Sierra Madre range. Not only are the facts as they appear today presented, but I have deemed it of interest to give a few pictorial and descriptive pages showing the road while under construction, and illustrating some of the difficulties which have been so successfully overcome.

I have written enthusiastically, but in every case truthfully. My undisguised love for the Crown of the San Gabriel Valley and her protecting Mother Mountains is such, that I have yet to find either of them in a mood or aspect which fails to please or delight me. From those who learn to love this region as I love it I am convinced that instead of receiving rebukes for undue enthusiasm and exaggeration of statement I shall hear the oft-repeated but never trite: "Not half has been told."

G. Wharton James.

Echo Mountain, Los Angeles Co., California.

Mount Lowe Railway.

PASADENA.

No poet's dream, painter's fancy, monk's ecstatic vision, musician's tone-picture, opium eater's exalted phantasy; no scene in the long fabled, beautiful Atlantis, or glorious vista seen by enraptured prophetic vision, ever surpassed what the eye actually gazes upon, as it surveys Pasadena, the Crown of the Valley of San Gabriel, in South California.

Artists, poets, authors, orators, travelers of all lands, as well as its cultured residents, alike bear tribute to its enduring charm. Indeed, so perfectly satisfying to so many needs are the atmospheric, climatic, and geographic conditions of this city—this coronet of diamonds on the brow of the San Gabriel that it is, and ever will be, world-famed.

Several conditions enter into the determination of a city's beauty, and these are either found within itself or in its location. A city may be situated in a location devoid of attractiveness, and yet be full of charm and delight. Other cities, viewed in conjunction with their location and surroundings, are strikingly beautiful and full of picturesqueness, which, when closely examined, become repulsive and depressing by their ugliness. Such a city is Constantinople. Seen from the Bosphorus one could imagine it the New Jerusalem let down from heaven, and a fit abode for the angels of God, but when one shut out from the surroundings of sea, mountain and verdure, walks its streets, he wonders at the ease with which he was deceived, and leaves Constantinople with his fondest illusions dispelled.

But Pasadena, both in location and within herself, is worthy of all the praise bestowed upon Constantinople as seen from the deck of the incoming vessel and before close contact has dispelled the first impressions.

It is a city of unequalled beauty. Standing in a commanding position, the key city of the San Gabriel Valley it has a large outlook over its sister cities and villages, and being almost immediately at the foot of the majestic Sierra Madre mountains, it thus enjoys close proximity to marvelous and sublime scenery, and is protected from the storms and the winds of the north.

Take a ride with me in *Midwinter*, and here is what your own description will be at the close of the day.

In every direction are trees: singly, in orchards, in groves, trees of olive, guava, eucalyptus, lime, almond, bay-wood, persimmon, pomegranate, cypress, fig, apricot, pepper, umbrella, peach, pear, prune, lemon and orange. The leaves are in every shade of green, the intense green of the olive almost black, when hidden from the sunshine. The apricots contribute

Residence of Professor T. S. C. Lowe, Orange Grove Avenue, Pasadena.

pink and white blossoms and whisper to us the secret of their exquisiteness, "the angels come and kiss us with the first dawnings of the morning." The eucalyptus and orange dazzle us with their bold beauty, for the one shows two or three different varieties of leaves, and the other presents blossom, green and ripe fruit on the same tree. And the peculiar richness of the groups of orange trees, who can comprehend, not having seen? Midas has been here, and his touch has made millions of green balls become golden, and they hang suspended amongst the marriage blossoms and leaves.

The granate-apple and the scarlet-fruited pepper tree stand side by side with the cypress, poplar, palm and cedar of Lebanon, whilst from yonder half-dozen magnolias the morning seductively draws a rich perfume, which a passing zephyr laughingly wafts around us for our enjoyment. The breeze awakens the bamboos and pampas grass which deferentially wave their white plumes in our presence.

Where are we? Surely in Japan, for here, with that peculiar orange redness of fruit, that cannot be mistaken, is the persimmon, and, land of surprises and imagination, it is *tete-a-tete* with an Arabian cactus.

No! It cannot be Japan, for yonder on the crest of the majestic mountains are the pines, firs and spruces of Norway and Sweden, and here are the yuccas of Mexico, the bananas of the Phillipine Islands, the guava and loquat of the semi-tropics, the oranges of Spain, the lemons of Portugal, the limes of Borneo and the dates of Turkey.

A strange land, indeed, where the flora is so diversified, and yet in nearly every case it all flourishes as well as if it were in its native soil and environment.

Then consider the atmosphere! Who can describe it? Pure, clear, serene, without a haze or a tremor, it reminds one of that "most pellucid air," through which Euripides describes the Athenians as "ever delicately marching."

And the climate! In other parts of the world latitude is the chief determining factor of climate, but in South California it seems to be altitude. For here in March 1894, in the San Gabriel valley, we are amidst ever-blooming fragrant flowers, whilst in the Sierra Madre mountains, thirty minutes ride away, snow covers the ground and sways the branches of the trees down to the earth.

Now look at the homes of Pasadena. No city in the world ever had clearer evidence of "foreordination" as a residence city. It is built upon a site rendered picturesque by the Arroyo Seco and the undulating slopes of the foot-hills, and thus by its diversified levels absolutely banishes monotony. Its residences, of course, are various, comprising the simple cottage of the laborer and the palace of the wealthy, but all are homes of fragrance and beauty.

The poorest peasant can vie with the millionaire in the profusion of his floral treasures, and the sweet odors that the sun extracts from these flowers, combined with the balmy richness distilled from a thousand shrubs and trees, give health as well as delight to the

PUBLIC LIBRARY, PASADENA.

senses of those who dwell within their reach.

Prof. Lowe owns a most beautiful residence, occupying a commanding situation on Orange Grove Avenue, in grounds, thirteen acres in extent, ornamented with a large variety of rare and exotic flowering plants, shrubs, and trees. In the library are many war mementos, photographs, etc., of the exciting times when Prof. Lowe skimmed above the clouds and through the air, while "shot and shell" pursued him from the foe beneath. There is the autograph letter from President Abraham Lincoln to Lieutenant-General Scott asking him to give further investigation to Professor Lowe's balloon plans. There are diplomas and certificates in number, from the leading scientific societies of the world and gold and silver medals of honor, amongst others one from the French Institute.

The public buildings of Pasadena are a wonder and a surprise even to those who are used to the magnificent structures of large Eastern cities. Its Public Library, though not a large structure, is, architecturally, a model building.

The Hotel Green, Hotel Raymond and Hotel Painter, are buildings that will bear comparison with the most renowned hotel structures of the world. The Green, especially, is the pride of Pasadenans. It was enlarged in 1893-4 by Col. G. G. Green, its enterprising owner, who expended over $300,000 in improving, refurnishing, etc., and it is now recognized as one of the leading hotels of the State.

The Raymond is too well-known throughout the tourist world to need description. It occupies an elevated site on the Raymond hill, which has been made into a perfect bower of beauty by trees, shrubs and flowers.

The Painter is a less pretentious structure, but its site near Altadena affords a beautiful outlook over the valley.

The school houses both public and private—together with the churches, add great architectural beauty to this flower-embowered city. All the public school buildings are model structures, and the Throop Polytechnic Institute, founded by the late lamented "Father" Throop,—has two magnificent buildings, especially designed and equipped for the manual, as well as mental, training of the young people of both sexes who are fortunate enough to be able to attend them.

The bank buildings, Board of Trade, and other business blocks all betoken a city of metropolitan character, and are indexes to the commercial prosperousness of the community.

The Grand Opera House Block is the grandest without question in Pasadena. It is a magnificent structure, and is owned by Professor Lowe. The Opera House is the finest west of the Mississippi and is managed by his son, Thaddeus Lowe, Jr. This magnificent block was purchased by Professor Lowe during the time of the depression which followed the South California boom some years ago, and when its original owners were so discouraged that they were about to tear it down and rebuild it in the form of houses or stores in another portion of the city. But, with that

keen foresight, which many people designate faith in the future prosperity of South California. Professor Lowe saw that the time would surely come when to have taken down this building would be regarded as a public calamity, hence its purchase, to remain as one of the objects of which Pasadena's citizens are proud.

In this block are the offices of the Mount Lowe Railway, together with the work-shops and stores, etc., of the Lowe Manufacturing Company in which the radiating gas stoves, and other of Professor Lowe's inventions in connection with the gas industry are manufactured.

The limited space of this article forbids more than the briefest mention of the other South California enterprises with which Professor Lowe is connected. Coming to Los Angeles in the year 1888, he entered the field of competition, and succeeded in giving the inhabitants of that city a better quality gas, at a much less price than they hitherto had been paying. He is now the largest individual stockholder in the Los Angeles Gas Lighting Company, and also the largest individual owner in the Pasadena Gas Works.

In the same year, he organized the Citizens' Bank in Los Angeles, and was for some time its President, until his arduous duties as President of the Mount Lowe Railway Company demanded more of his time, so that he resigned, but he is still the Vice President and one of the Directors. He is the President of the Los Angeles Safe Deposit & Trust Company, owning a major portion of the stock, and he is also one of the Directors of the Columbia Savings Bank, of which T. D. Stimson is President. In addition to this, he was one of the organizers and is a large stockholder in the Los Angeles Ice Manufacturing Company.

Considering these facts, and the still more important one that it is to his indomitable energy and mechanical genius the world is indebted for the Mount Lowe Railway, it is natural that considerable interest should center around the personality of Professor Lowe.

It is not my purpose here to present a biographical sketch of the distinguished aeronaut, scientific inventor and mountain railway builder, but simply to call attention to some of the important services he has rendered mankind, the notable enterprises besides the Mountain Railway with which his name is inseparably connected.

There are four things from which it will ever be impossible to dissever Professor Lowe's name, for they owe their existence to his brilliant and diverse genius. These are,

First: He originated and established the first practical system of aeronautic observations for war purposes, and he was also the first to utilize the telegraph for establishing communication between the earth and the balloon in the air. By this means he made it possible to discover the movements of the enemy and give accurate information of them at the exact time they were being made. The story of how he became interested in the balloon is interestingly told in the lecture delivered by Professor Lowe before the Unity Club of Los Angeles, January 24th, 1891.

PROFESSOR T. S. C. LOWE

"From living in high altitudes, I had observed that there are often very different air currents in the valleys from those which exist in the upper atmosphere. From the recognition of this simple fact, it occurred to me that if a system of observations could be inaugurated by means of which the varying atmospheric conditions existing in different parts of the country could all be telegraphed to a competent person in Washington and then carefully collated, weather forecasts could then be made from them and telegraphically distributed throughout the country, to the great advantage of our agricultural and other interests. To the agriculturist these forecasts would give notice of weather changes, which, if he knew were to occur, would be of great benefit to him. To the marine interests these forecasts would be more important still, for, giving notice of threatened storms, vessels would thus be prevented from leaving shore at times which might prove disastrous.

My idea was the organizing of a Weather Bureau exactly after the plan now followed by the government, and I might here remark that it was owing to my investigations and the laying of my plans before Gen. Albert Myer, Chief Signal officer of the army, at various times during my war service, as well as after the war closed, that at least, in a great measure, hastened the establishing of the bureau, and I believe myself to be the first to suggest such a bureau for the making of weather forecasts.

For some time I continued my experiments studying the currents on the surface of the earth, but soon being desirous of investigating the upper air currents, which I could see by watching the various strata of clouds, were often diverse from the earth currents, the balloon occurred to my mind as the only possible vehicle for making the necessary investigations.

Accordingly, in the year 1858, I constructed a balloon and made a number of ascensions and the result of these was that I discovered the existence of an upper air current which invariably moved eastward, with but slight variations, no matter how diverse the surface currents might be. I then opened up communication with Prof. Joseph Henry, of the Smithsonian Institution, hoping through him to be able to interest the government to aid in the carrying out of my plan. As soon as the results of my experiments were made known to him, he became very much interested. A number of merchants also of the eastern cities were equally interested in the work of the balloon, for as in those days there was no electric telegraph communication under the ocean between this country and Europe, as there is now, the merchants were exceedingly anxious to find a method of tranportation which would convey important mercantile news ahead of the steamers.

Personally, I was not much interested in the object of the merchants except in as far as it might produce means to enable me to pursue my further investigations. At the same time, I was desirous of testing the air currents over the ocean to see whether the same conditions existed there as over the land.

MOUNT LOWE RAILWAY.

Prof. Henry, however, with that large kindly-heartedness that characterized the man, did not wish to encourage a project which appeared to him and others to be perilous to the lives of those engaged in it. So he advised that I go West with my balloon, make an ascent when the earth currents were blowing strongly to the west, and then, if when reaching the upper currents I sailed across the continent east, the existence of this eastward current which I claimed did exist would be sufficiently demonstrated to justify his urging the Government to aid me in my Atlantic experiments. I had already constructed for this Atlantic trip the largest aerostadt ever made, and which never since has been approached in size or equipment, and with which I had safely lifted from the earth, including its own weight, 16 tons, so that I was thoroughly convinced that I could safely convey across the Atlantic all the materials I required for comfort and safety. Not only was this balloon to carry ample instruments, provisions for the crew, and all the implements, etc., required for observation, and the manipulation of the balloon, but also a full-rigged life-boat schooner built of light steel plates with air tight compartments.

Acceding to Prof. Henry's request, however, I left this large balloon and taking my smaller experimental balloon went to Cincinnati, and for about a month waited for conditions to be exactly as I desired before making the ascent. The newspapers took a great deal of interest in the project, some of them speaking in the most favorable terms of the work, and others laughingly referring to it. At last the conditions were highly favorable for the experiment, the surface currents moving rapidly westward, and accordingly after learning by telegraph that the same conditions existed so far east as Washington, I made the ascent at 3 o'clock of the morning of April 20th, 1861. Some of the newspapers amusingly stated after I had ascended that the balloon which had gone up for the purpose of demonstrating the existence of an upper air current which invariably flowed eastward, when last seen, was rapidly sailing west. But when later in the morning at daylight, a telegraphic dispatch was sent all over the country from Falmouth, Ky., saying that a large balloon had been seen high up in the air rapidly moving eastward, all who saw the dispatch and knew of my discovery were convinced of the correctness of my former deductions.

In crossing over the Alleghanies a deep current of air flowing between these mountains and the Blue Ridge drew the balloon slightly southward, although had it been sufficiently large so I could have kept high enough to remain in the undisturbed flow of the eastward current, this surface disturbance would not have affected my movements. The result was that I landed in South Carolina, a short distance from the line of North Carolina nearly in a due east direction from Cincinnati.

In crossing over Virginia I could distinctly hear the cannonading which told the story that the Virginians were celebrating the fact of their secession. South Carolina had already gone out of the Union, and the descent of my balloon caused a great deal of excitement, it being only eight days after the attack on Fort Sumter. I was looked upon as a Federal spy, and was arrested and locked up in Columbia jail. Indeed, it is asserted on good authority that I was the first prisoner of war captured by the South during the civil war.

Not desiring to be shot as a spy, I sent for the president of the South Carolina college, and he satisfactorily explained to the authorities that he was familiar with the purpose of my balloon experiments, which at that time had nothing to do with the army, and at the solicitation of himself and faculty, I was released. Mayor Boatright of Columbia then accorded me the freedom of the city and a letter bearing the city seal asking a safe conduct for me through "the Confederate states of North America." The incidents for the next five days and nights were as interesting as any in the whole course of my life. I heard a number of speeches against the Union; I saw the trains loaded with Union families going west to get out of the Confederacy, as all communication to the north was cut off by Confederate forces at Manassas Junction, and the silence that generally prevailed was striking in the extreme.

As I passed through Tennessee I learned, through means that would be quite interesting to relate had I time, the fact that that state had gone out of the Union in secret session. This I communicated to President Lincoln two weeks before it became authentically known from the state.

On my arrival at Cincinnati I found people very much interested in the result of my experiments, but I was desirous of urging on my Atlantic trip, and was both surprised and disappointed when I received a dispatch from Secretary Chase saying that President Lincoln desired to consult with me in regard to organizing a balloon service for the U. S. army. Prof. Henry and the friends upon whom I had relied for assistance to carry out my Atlantic plans positively refused to aid me further until the country was at peace. They argued that, as the country desired and needed my services, my own personal plans ought to be subservient to the wishes of the government. Accordingly I went to Washington, consulted with President Lincoln and the military authorities, and the result was that through the aid of the President I finally organized the Aeronautic Corps of the U. S. army.

I have devoted considerable space to this quotation from Professor Lowe's lecture, but the important historical facts therein contained, being thus presented for the first time, afford ample justification. To resume the brief enumeration of his labors:

Second: He invented, made and put into successful operation the first practical ice making machine ever manufactured, and yet, so far was he in advance of the times that his original patents had expired before the Ice Machine came into general use. His machine, however, was as perfect in principle and mechanical construction as any of those made in the present day and was as successful in the manufacture of ice and artificial refrigeration. And it was because he thus clearly demonstrated the feasibility of this invention that other manufacturers followed in his wake and patented what was already, to him, an old story.

Third: He originated, and put into successful operation the first practical method of producing illuminating water gas which is now used all over the civilized world. Fully two-thirds of all the gas made in the United States is made by this process, and a reference to any of the Gas Journals, whether of the past or present time, will show by the constant allusions to the "Lowe Process," and the and the many tributes paid to the inventor's ability and skill, how valuable and important his inventions in this regard are esteemed.

Fourth: The three above mentioned beneficial inventions entitled Professor Lowe to rank as a man who has lived for the good of his fellow-men, but I feel safe in saying that his fourth and last work, will prove of greater benefit to mankind in general than any or all of the others. To him the world owes the

Electric Railway system of Mountain climbing which will entirely displace the old and cumbersome locomotive-and-cog-wheel-method of reaching Mountain heights. He has thus opened up to the easy enjoyment of thousands, what they, through physical inability would never have been able to see, and thus by bringing them in contact with Nature's secret recesses, where vigor, strength and health are kept in abundant store has entitled himself to the gratitude of many whose lives will be lengthened through his labors.

These four great inventions unquestionably mark epochs in their particular lines as important as the discoveries of Copernicus in astronomy, Newton in gravitation, Linnaeus in botany or Stevenson in locomotive engineering, for they will unquestionably remain as the line of demarkation separating the old from the new. And it is not only just to remember that, no matter what improvements or alterations may be made, the first principles originated in the active and prolific brain of Professor T. S. C. Lowe.

Will Lieut! Gen'l Scott please [...] Professor Lowe over now about his balloon?

July 25, 1861,

A Lincoln

Fac-simile of the autograph card given to Prof. T. S. C. Lowe by President Lincoln, asking Lieut. General Scott to see Prof. Lowe "once more" about his balloon.

LEAVING ALTADENA FOR THE SIERRA MADRE MOUNTAINS DURING THE CONSTRUCTION OF THE
MOUNT LOWE RAILWAY.

Up to The Sierra Madre Mountains.

What is the setting of the exquisite picture I have attempted in the foregoing pages to describe?

Pasadena has a background of beauty, glory and majesty seldom equalled. This background is a peerless range of mountains the Appenines, the Pasadena Alps, and, as its name implies, it is a sheltering mother, protecting its sun-kissed and flower-bedecked garden of the Lord from the stern winds which blow so penetratingly in other regions. Picturesque and bold it stands, seamed with deep canyons, wooded gorges and precipitous cliffs, Its serrated summits look near enough for us to reach them by walking in an hour, for the transparent atmosphere deceives us. Its peaks are higher than the highest peaks of the White Mountains, and we are instinctively seized with an uncontrollable desire to scale them and look down upon the fair panorama beneath.

"Contrary to many of the mountain views afforded the transcontinental traveler, this semi-crescent sweep of fifty miles in length, approximating in its adjacent ranges an elevation of ten or eleven thousand feet, fulfills one's ideal of what a mountain range should be. The summits are often robed in the lofty splendor of snow-white mantles contrasting strongly with the permanent dark evergreen forests of the central ranges."

This chain of mountains runs transversely across Southern California, near the 34th parallel of latitude. Along its southern foothills are the flourishing orange groves of the beautiful cities of Los Angeles, Pasadena, San Gabriel, Monrovia, Duarte, Azusa, Pomona, Cucamonga, Rialto, San Bernardino and Redlands. A little further south, but within view of the mountains, are the prolific orchards of the equally beautiful Riverside, Arlington, Puente, Orange, Santa Ana, Anaheim, Fullerton, Rivera and Whittier.

The Los Angeles Terminal Railway directly connects with the Mount Lowe Railway at Altadena Junction, where, surrounded by orange groves and flower gardens, the depot stands. The accompanying engraving shows the temporary method used for conveying Prof. Lowe's guests during the period of construction. The freight-car has an immediate background of orange trees, while in the distance, on the right of the engraving can dimly be seen the grade of the Great Cable Incline on Echo Mountain.

But now, well-equipped passenger cars, fitted up with the most approved electric power speed up Lake Avenue, and in a few minutes land passengers at the "White Chariots" of the Great Cable Incline, which latter has truthfully been designated "the most wonderful railway of the world."

Here at Altadena, also, are located the gas engines, working the electric dynamos which supply power for operating the Trolley Road to Rubio Amphitheater. These consist of two 60-horse-power and one 100-horse-power gas engines, with a capacity much larger than their specified amount.

Starting for the Summit from Rubio Canyon before the Completion of the Mount Lowe Railway to Echo Mountain.

MOUNT LOWE RAILWAY.

"Bound for the Summit" before the completion of the Road.

Leaving Altadena Junction the electric car heads directly for the mountains, up Lake Avenue for about a mile, then, crossing the high mesa upon which the poppies —*the Copa de Oro* of the Spaniards grow in profusion, enters Rubio Canyon. This mesa is an historic spot having been named by the sailors of the pioneer navigator, Cabrillo, Cape Floral. The flaming and gorgeous poppies reflecting the brilliant sunlight made a spectacle of dazzling gold which was clearly seen sixty miles out at sea,—hence the name.

As one looks up from this starting point to Echo Mountain, crowned by several substantial buildings, the name, mountain, seems a misnomer, for it appears only an abutment to the mountains. And although so close, it is almost impossible to realize that it is separated, except in one spot, from the main range by a canyon a thousand feet deep and half a mile wide.

Now the car enters Rubio Canyon. At its mouth it is broad, and though rugged, its slopes are neither imposing nor precipitous; but after crossing the first bridge, the scenery begins rapidly to change. This bridge is built in a substantial manner, of the same sized timbers as those used in the bridges of the Santa Fe system, so that we journey along without the slightest sense of insecurity or danger. Eleven of these bridges are crossed in the two and a half miles' ride to Rubio pavilion. The road passes through one cut in the solid granite rock, which had to be made by men suspended by ropes from above. Here, dangling in mid-air, they drilled the holes, and, filling them with powder, were drawn up before the explosion took place. Hence, we are not surprised to find ourselves in romantic defiles, the slopes growing steeper and more closely confined as we ascend. Our road curves and twines around, leading us sometimes to wonder where we can possibly be going. The car again and again seems heading directly for the edge of the precipice, but, at the danger-point, it easily slips around the jutting crags and climbs merrily on.

The sides of the canyon are richly clothed with variegated shrubs, flowers and trees, enlivened by hundreds of the stately and beautiful "yuccas," "Spanish-bayonets," whose waxen and and bell-like white flowers, reflecting the brilliant sunlight suggested to the imaginative Spanish priests the poetic name Candlestick of our Lord.

These, and many other sights, were thoroughly enjoyed by the party pictured on the opposite page, who were "bound for the summit" before the completion of the railway. The construction trails over which they rode to Echo Mountain are now permanently closed and the only "open sesame" to the grand and glorious nature panorama exhibited from Echo Mountain is the Great Cable Incline.

Among the Maples and Sycamores in Rubio Canyon.

Among the Maples and Sycamores in Rubio Canyon.

Immediately on entering Rubio Canyon the visitor is charmed and surprised with the richness of the verdure, the trees, shrubs and flowers that greet his eye. From the valley the mountains seemed barren, now we learn that they are fairly covered with mountain mahogany, lilac, holly, and other chapparal, whilst in the deeper canyons pines, spruces, bays, maples, sycamores and live oaks flourish in large numbers. Ferns, mosses and trailing vines in profusion and variety cover the rocks, whilst the more delicate species

"The witching tangle of the maiden-hair,
The sweet grace of the gold and silver ferns,
The nodding coffee-fern with beauty rare"

seek shelter in hidden nooks, whose perfect solitude is only penetrated by the lover and the enthusiast.

As the road in Rubio Canyon curves it affords many beautiful views of the valley we are leaving behind, but none so rich and perfect as the one we get from Lookout Point. Here, the peculiar conformation of the canyon presents the scene below in a natural framework of gray rock, rich trees and azure sky.

Look at it!

Orchards, vineyards, grain fields, eucalyptus groves, "walnut walks, fig tree lanes," parks, gardens and grounds. Mansions of princely creation, with architecture borrowed from the world's best models, surrounded or fronted by lawn and terrace, adorned with statuary, shrubs and flowers, from every quarter of the globe. Streets, made into gardens by red fruited pepper, graceful umbrella and oriental palm, whilst here, and there, and everywhere are cottages fairly smothered in a profusion of roses. One of God's choicest mosaics, made instinct with the life of His children. And while the eye is drinking this superb scene in to the full, exclamations of delight and surprise arrest our attention. We turn around and there, in full view, is Hotel Rubio, the Music Hall and the Great Cable Incline.

AMONG THE FERNS IN RUBIO CANYON.

Electric Trolley Cars Connecting with Great Cable Incline at Hotel Rubio.

MOUNT LOWE RAILWAY.

HOTEL RUBIO.

Hotel Rubio is a most unique structure. It is built in the heart of Rubio Canyon, and above it is the immense platform bridging the canyon on which stands the Music Hall, pronounced by the Chevalier de Konski, pianist to the Emperor of Germany, "the most perfect building to play in possible to be conceived."

The dining room is elegant and commodious, its length being about 110 feet by 35 feet broad. There is not a pillar or post to obstruct the view in this well-proportioned room, and its beauty is enhanced by being finished in the natural woods. Pure mountain water from the celebrated Maple Springs is used on the tables and for all culinary purposes. It is a chemically pure water and aids digestion in a remarkable manner.

During the seasons when evening trains are run, whether on special occasions, tri-weekly or each evening, superbly illustrated lectures of travel are given in the Music Hall. Concerts, balls, parties, and other entertainments are also often given, and thus every provision is made for the pleasure of the guests.

Hotel Rubio and the Music Hall are in the Great Rocky Amphitheater, a natural basin, formed of the towering mountain sides which slope back and up towards the sky. It is a romantic, beautiful and picturesque spot, 2200 feet above sea level.

At Hotel Rubio the electric trolley cars of the Mount Lowe Railway from Altadena Junction connect with the "White Chariots" of the Great Cable Incline for Echo Mountain and the higher ranges of Mount Lowe.

Standing on Rubio Platform, the visitor gets his first full view of the Great Cable Incline. From the valley even from cities as far away as Los Angeles he may have seen the electric lights, which at night illuminate this mountain railway and show its steep grade, but now he stands before it and takes in its marvelous features in one view. At least he imagines he does. But his view is by no means complete. Only by riding over it can all its wondrousness be comprehended. He will then be surprised to learn that his view from below only comprised about two-thirds of its height, the angle of inclination being such that the fifty-eight and forty-eight per cent. grades are not visible from the foot. He will stand and watch the cars ascending and descending almost after the fashion of "the old oaken-buckets" of boyhood's days, and see with wonder the readiness with which the cars turn out at the midway point, without any switchman to guide them, thus solving the engineer's problem of sixty years or more, viz: how to make two cars pass on the same track without frogs, switches, etc. He will listen to the unanimous exclamations of delight the returning passengers give expression to, and then, as every other visitor has done, will take his seat and soar upwards in a manner he never before had conceived possible.

Prof. Lowe and Guests at Suspended Boulder in Rubio Canyon.

MOUNT LOWE RAILWAY

On the Suspended Boulder in Rubio Canyon.

The Mount Lowe Railway was not opened to the public until Tuesday, July 1, 1893, but on Saturday, July 1, a select number of the distinguished citizens of Los Angeles and Pasadena were invited to inspect the work accomplished, and, after a careful and extended survey of the electric road, the Great Cable Incline and the plank walks and staircases which render the beauties of Rubio Canyon accessible, President Lowe entertained his guests with an elaborate banquet at Hotel Rubio.

The accompanying engraving is made from a photograph which happily caught Prof. Lowe standing on the Suspended Boulder, addressing his guests.

This Boulder is but one of many objects of interest in Rubio Canyon, including Fern Glens, Moss Grottoes, Peculiar Stone Formations, Grand Chasms, Ribbon Rock, Thalehaha and nine other exquisitely beautiful Water-Falls.

Just below the Suspended Boulder is Mirror Lake. It extends across the complete width of the canyon, which somewhat narrows at this point, and reaches for quite a little distance, being bridged by the plank-walk leading to the Grand Chasm and Thalehaha Falls. The exquisite reflections of the trees, shrubs and towering rocks, together with the electric lights and Japanese lanterns at night, give to Mirror Lake an indescribable charm which always fascinates and attracts.

Few places, if any, of natural interest, have so rapidly bounded into the favor of the public. Twenty thousand persons visited it in the first four months it was opened, viz.: from July 1 to the end of October, and many of these visitors have repeated the trip ten or a dozen times. Its beauties grow more attractive the more one becomes familiar with them, and, therefore, not only will it be a place for tourists to visit, but it will also be a popular resort for the local population, which is prosperous enough to create a demand for such a high-class pleasure resort and adequately sustain it.

The importance of the figures above given and the phenomenal success they record will be observed, when it is considered that the opening of the road took place with four potent influences at work against it, viz.: 1. The financial depression was at its worst and people were afraid of spending money for anything but necessities. 2. A large number of the local population had already gone to the World's Fair. 3. Many others had availed themselves of the reduced railroad rates to visit their friends in the East; and, 4. The exodus from the cities and valley towns had already taken place to the seaside. Hundreds of families had located there who would have preferred to spend a portion of their summer holidays in the mountains had the railway been in operation.

These facts are thus presented in order that the success the road has attained may be understood, and, also, that the expectations as to its future prosperity when conditions are more favorable, times improved, and the people have become accustomed to visiting it, may not be regarded as exaggerations, but as the legitimate deductions of reason from accomplished facts.

Great Cable Incline of Mount Lowe Railway.

MOUNT LOWE RAILWAY

GREAT CABLE INCLINE.

This marvellous piece of railroad engineering has called forth the unstinted praise of many eminent engineers. The scientific press has been unanimous in expatiating upon its unique features and designates it "the greatest mountain railway enterprise in existence," and says "the engineering problems have been solved in a manner to challenge our admiration."

This Incline extends from Rubio Pavilion, 2,200 feet above the sea, to the summit of Echo Mountain, 3,500 feet in altitude. It is upwards of 3,000 feet in length, and makes a direct ascent of about 1,300 feet.

The cars are permanently attached to an endless cable, and are so balanced, that in ascending and descending, they pass each other at an automatic turnout, exactly midway on the Incline.

The cable is of the finest steel and was thoroughly tested to a strain of one hundred tons, and, as under any circumstances the loaded cars will never exceed five tons, its absolute safety is at once apparent.

The view, in ascending, is indescribably grand. The motion is smooth and easy as if soaring to the clouds on the wings of an eagle. Almost noiselessly the car glides upwards, and nothing distracts the attention of passengers from the picturesque sweetness and serene majesty of the scene.

At first, the mountains composing Rubio Amphitheater appear to rise with the car, and yet the view enlarges every moment. Passing through Granite Gorge,—an immense cut in the mountain slope, where all the workmen who could possibly be crowded upon the mass were engaged for eight long months before a single tie could be laid, over the Macpherson Trestle,—an immense bridge, 100 feet higher at one end than the other—the San Gabriel Valley begins to unfold its incomparable charms, and, as the elevation grows higher, the view expands and enlarges, until, on reaching the summit of Echo Mountain, and standing on one of the verandas of Echo Mountain House, the whole scene is presented in its full glory, to the entrancing delight of all who behold it.

As visitors ride up this Great Incline, how few of them dream of the arduous labor it represents. Not only were the ordinary difficulties of railroad building to overcome, but the grade was such, that burros had to carry cement and water for building the walls and buttresses, which, in places, were necessary, ere the track could be laid, and, as there were many points where not even burros could climb in safety, men carried the required materials on their shoulders. It will be apparent, therefore, to the least initiated, how much labor and cost were expended in its construction, and yet, up to the time of laying the last rail it was the money, energy and engineering skill of one man who accomplished it, when the great majority, with less foresight and courage, regarded the undertaking as well nigh impossible.

Granite Gorge on Great Cable Incline of Mount Lowe Railway.

MOUNT LOWE RAILWAY.

Granite Gorge, Macpherson Trestle, and Loading the Construction Car

The engraving on the opposite, and those on the two following pages, illustrate respectively two scenes on the Great Cable Incline, and one of the daily occurrences during the latter part of its construction. Soon after leaving Hotel Rubio the "White Chariot" enters Granite Gorge, a cut through the solid mountain slope so difficult to undertake as to require the labor of all the men that could be placed upon it for eight months before a single tie or rail could be laid. The grade of the Incline being so steep the work could only be accomplished at the upper end, the debris being carried out backwards and dumped into the canyon below. This Gorge affords a most interesting study in "folding" to the geologist, and when its lesson is read a key is given to the history of the whole range.

Passing through Granite Gorge the rumbling of the car wheels denotes that we are on a trestle bridge.

The great trestle on the line of the White Mountain Railroad received the name of "Frankenstein" in honor of the engineer of the road, and Professor Lowe deemed it appropriate to name this far more important bridge the "Macpherson trestle," in honor of the indefatigable labors and engineering skill of his chief engineer. It is a singular structure, and, if placed on level ground would not only excite wonder and amazement, but curiosity as to where it could possibly be used, for, in its length of a little over 200 feet it makes an ascent of over 100 feet, and the unique appearance of a bridge a hundred feet higher at one end than the other can better be imagined than described. The Construction Car which is being loaded with supplies, is represented in this engraving, conveying a load of lumber to the summit of Echo Mountain for building purposes.

In this connection let me answer viz.: "How did you get the Cable and all the Operating Machinery of the Incline in place?"

When the grading of the Incline was completed, supports, on which were wheels, were fastened into the mountain on the side of the roadbed. At the same time, the great windlass, which was made in sections below, together with a heavy manilla rope, were packed on burros to the summit of Echo Mountain. As soon as the windlass was in place, the rope was securely fastened to it and let down over the wheels to the bottom of the Incline, where the ends of the rope and the steel construction cable were firmly united. The horses attached to the hoisting apparatus were then set in motion, and, as the drum revolved the cable was drawn up. This was of sufficient strength for all the purposes of construction, and for hauling up the vast amount of machinery necessary for working the monster passenger cable, and, finally, this latter cable itself.

As soon as this great cable was in position, one of the passenger cars was attached to it, and with the powerful electric motor now used in operating this cable, was drawn to the summit when the second car was attached at the bottom and everything was ready for the conveyance of passengers. An illustration on a subsequent page shows the machinery used during construction.

Loading Construction Car at the Foot of Great Cable Incline.

Construction Car Loaded with Lumber on Macpherson Trestle Ascending the Great Cable Incline.

ECHO MOUNTAIN HOUSE.—White Chariot on the 48 per cent. Grade of the C...

MOUNT LOWE RAILWAY.

White Chariot and Echo Mountain Chalet.

The grade of the Great Cable Incline begins at 60 per cent. After passing the turnout it is 62 per cent. for quite a distance, then it makes two "buckles," one to 58 per cent., and on nearing the summit to 48 per cent.

The engraving shows one of the "White Chariots" as the Incline Cars have not inappropriately been named, on the 48 per cent. grade, with the Chalet on Echo Mountain above in the background. The cars are so arranged as to keep passengers always on the level, regardless of the steep grades of the Incline. They are uncovered so as to afford a perfectly unobstructed view in every possible direction, and, as a rule, the weather is so fine and propitious that no inconvenience is experienced, as would be expected in a more rigorous climate.

Echo Mountain gains its name from the unequalled echoes heard from the summit. Standing on the edge of Echo Canyon, the firing of a rifle, the blowing of a bugle, shouting, or hallooing produces echoes, clear, distinct, and of long continuance.

The Chalet is a romantically situated hotel, perched on the slope of Echo Mountain and is as cosy and home-like a resting-place as can anywhere be found. But as a hotel it holds second place to the great Echo Mountain House, which, in its healthful conditions, its artistic and pleasurable location, its unique and superb views surpasses any other hotel in the world. The passengers on the Great Cable Incline land directly on the veranda of this superb hotel. It has a double frontage, South East and North West, the two portions meeting in a central hall which is surmounted by an elegant dome, in turn overtopped by a flagstaff from which the Stars and Stripes ever proudly float.

The climate of Echo Mountain is equable and delightful during the entire year. When clouds and fogs obstruct the vision and render residence somewhat uncomfortable in the valley, the mountain is invariably bathed in sunshine, with a dry air pervading the atmosphere. One of the most beautiful sights from Echo Mountain House is to see the fog or cloud, like a white sea, hiding all but a few pinnacles and islands of the valley beneath, and, as the sun shines upon it, lighting it up into a fleecy brilliancy, and often disclosing all the colors of the rainbow, entirely different from any other earthly scene.

The experience of several seasons has demonstrated that on Echo Mountain the air is warmer in winter and cooler in summer than in the valley beneath, and no matter how warm it may be in the valley, there is always a cool breeze on the verandas of Echo Mountain House. Thus it will be noticed by those who desire an equable climate, that here it can be obtained, for the variations of temperature are comparatively slight throughout the entire year.

Here, overlooking the picturesque and beautiful San Gabriel and Los Angeles valleys, with their numerous villages, towns, and cities, the long stretch of gray beach, the placid ocean and its numerous islands, the whole scene surrounded by virgin-white mountain peaks, soothed by the refreshing snow-kissed zephyrs, one may while the happy hours away in delicious languor and restoring restfulness.

The sunrises and sunsets as viewed from Echo Mountain are as gorgeously beautiful as at those places rendered famous by brilliant and rhetorical verse. The visitor should invariably stay over night at Echo Mountain to enjoy these surpassingly glorious scenes.

LOWE OBSERVATORY.

As is well known Professor Lowe has always kept in view his pledge, long-ago made, to build and equip an astronomical observatory on the Sierra Madre mountains that would be second to no observatory in the world, in offering facilities to the astronomer for the performance of good work. In accordance with that pledge the temporary observatory is now erected on Echo Mountain. The engraving below is not a representation of the Echo Mountain strument with which he is now searching the heavens is a 16-inch refractor, made, in his best days by Alvan Clark, the veteran lens-maker of Cambridgeport, Mass., and it is, according to the maker's testimony, the best glass he ever made of its size. At the close of the summer it is confidently anticipated that the remaining section of the Mount Lowe Railway to the summit of Mount Lowe will be completed, and then the large 37½-inch

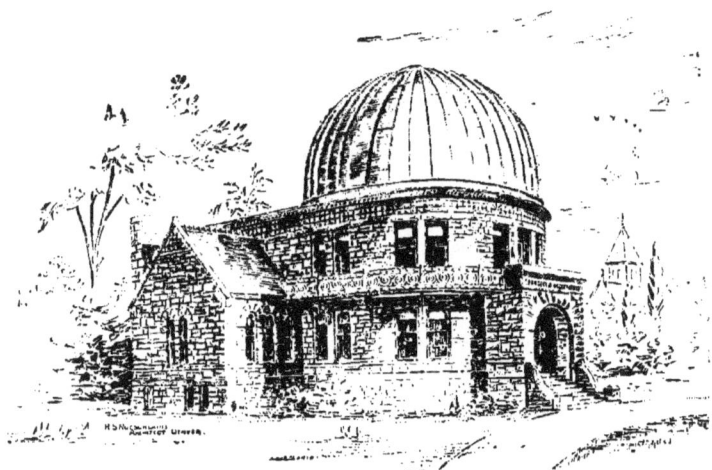

tain Observatory but serves to show, somewhat, the style of one of the buildings on the Summit of Mount Lowe when the completed Observatory plan of Professor Lowe is carried out.

Dr. Lewis Swift, formerly of the Warner Observatory of Rochester, N. Y., the eminent astronomer—the "indefatigable comet-seeker" as his brother astronomers term him, has charge of the observatory. The in- reflecting telescope for photographic work, together with three other telescopes, will be erected on the highest crest of the Monarch of the Sierra Madre range, and thus an astronomical observatory founded, 2000 feet higher than the Lick Observatory, in a climate much superior to that possessed by Mount Hamilton, and with a survey of a portion of the Stellar zone as yet unexplored.

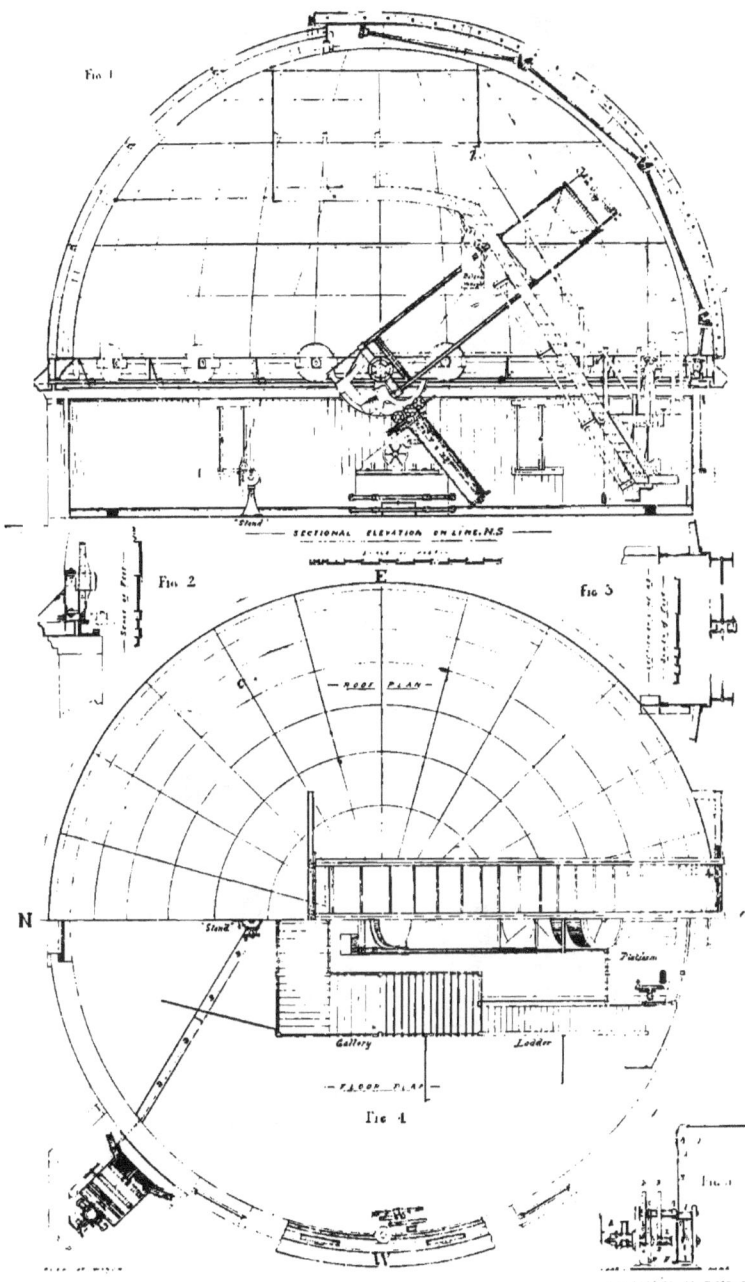

Fig. 1

Fig. 2

Fig. 3

SECTIONAL ELEVATION ON LINE N.S

ROOF PLAN

E

N

Stand

Platform

Gallery

Ladder

FLOOR PLAN

Fig. 4

Ground and Interior Plan of the Observatory for the 37½ inch Reflecting Telescope
to be placed on Mount Lowe.

Electrical Machinery for Operating the Great Cable Incline of the Mount Lowe Railway.

Operating Machinery of the Great Cable Incline.

Like so many other things in connection with the Mount Lowe Railway, the machinery is unique and unlike anything ever before constructed. The power is generated by two methods, viz.: 1. By water wheels and dynamos situated at Hotel Rubio, the water flowing through pipes from the reservoir on Echo Mountain, (which is supplied from a still higher level), and, 2. by immense gas engines and dynamos at Altadena Junction, where the power house is situated.

These gas engines are used to supplement the water power, should there be a dry season, and they, solely, for the first nine months, were used for operating the Electric and Cable Incline Cars, and carrying the large number of passengers who have patronized the road.

In either case the electric power is transmitted by large copper conductors to the Echo Mountain power house, supplying current to the 100 horse power electric motor, which makes 800 revolutions per minute. Then by a series of gears the revolutions are reduced from 800 to 17 per minute, which is the speed at which the massive grip-sheave turns. The grip-sheave consists of a tremendously heavy wheel, on which about 70 automatic steel jaws are affixed. As the wheel revolves, these jaws close and grip the endless cable, to which the cars are permanently attached, and thus are they raised or lowered as occasion requires. By this method there is practically no wear whatever on the cable. It is not strained and chafed by the constant operation of gripping as on the Street Railway Cars where the inertia of trains of cars of many tons' weight has to be overcome by the gripping of the ever moving cable.

Every safety device and appliance of known utility that could be here used has been placed upon the machinery and thoroughly tested, so that the unanimous verdict of the many eminent engineers who have scientifically examined in detail the machinery and its working is a deserved tribute to the foresight of Prof. Lowe and his engineers. That verdict is, that "it is the safest railroad ever constructed; the possibilty of accident is reduced to a lower minimum than on any cable, electric, or steam system in the world."

Standing on the Hotel veranda or at the power house on Echo Mountain one can look directly down upon the electric cars leaving Altadena Junction on their way to Rubio Canyon. One portion of Lake Avenue, up which they pass, is the steepest part of the whole electric trolley system, having a grade of 8½ per cent., whilst in no other portion of the line, even that already surveyed and now being graded from Echo Mountain to the summit of Mount Lowe, does it exceed 7½ per cent.

The use of water in generating power for the whole of the Mount Lowe Railway system is a great desideratum, for it reduces the expenses of operation to the lowest possible minimum.

By means of reservoirs already constructed, a sufficiency of water can be stored for all practical purposes, and these reservoirs being at different elevations allow the same water to be used again and again in the generation of power.

On Bridle Road in Castle Canyon, on the "Mount Lowe Eight."

MOUNT LOWE RAILWAY.

On the "Mount Lowe Eight."

To ride on well constructed bridle roads up mountain slopes, winding in and out on diversified paths, through and by bowers of fragrant trees, shrubs and flowers, looking *up* through towering pines to majestic cliffs and ponderous rocks, looking *down* into the depths of vast canyons, where deer find shady coverts, and looking *out* upon scenes of perfect beauty and sublimity—these things fill the body with vigor and buoyant enthusiasm, and the mind with lasting pictures of increasing interest.

Realizing this, Professor Lowe has had constructed more than thirty miles of wide and easy-graded bridle roads radiating from Echo Mountain to all the higher peaks and summits of the range. The most important sections of these roads are known as the "Mount Lowe Eight," for, in making the complete ride to the summit of Mount Lowe from Echo Mountain and return, the figure "eight" is described, the rider only crossing his own path in one place, and nowhere else riding twice on the same road. These roads were carefully constructed so as to include all the scenic portions of the mountains, and also to afford the grandest outlooks upon the valleys and more distant scenery. They also lead to the points and summits selected as the sites of the two Observatories,—astronomical and meteorological,—soon to be established.

A large corral is located on Echo Mountain, in which horses, mules and burros are kept for the use of visitors—whether ladies, gentlemen or children—who desire to make this trip. It is a perfectly easy trip for anyone to make, even ladies and children having gone unattended to the summit of Mount Lowe and return with comfort and safety.

Competent guides are always to be had on Echo Mountain.

The ride over the "Mount Lowe Eight" includes Castle Canyon, so named because of the rows of rocks which line its sides, resembling castles, towers, pagodas, minarets and temples, Mount Lowe Saddle, a ridge connecting the front and rear ranges, where all the bridle, electric, and sleighing roads unite.

Grand Basin, a vast wide-spreading, rocky, tree-clad area of thousands of acres, (with a mountain over 2000 feet high, upon the summit of which the visitor on Mount Lowe can look down several thousand feet), embraced in its wide-spreading reach. Great Bear Canyon, rocky, precipitous, thrilling 3000 feet or more in depth and yet so lined with trees as to be a perfect bower of beauty, Sunset Point, where the last rays of the setting sun caressingly linger each day, and Los Flores and Millard Canyons. Such a mountain ride as this the world nowhere else affords.

Geologically it is interesting beyond measure, for, such have been the changes in this range in the past centuries, that strata, overturned, twisted, curved and tilted in every conceivable way, are opened up for fullest inspection.

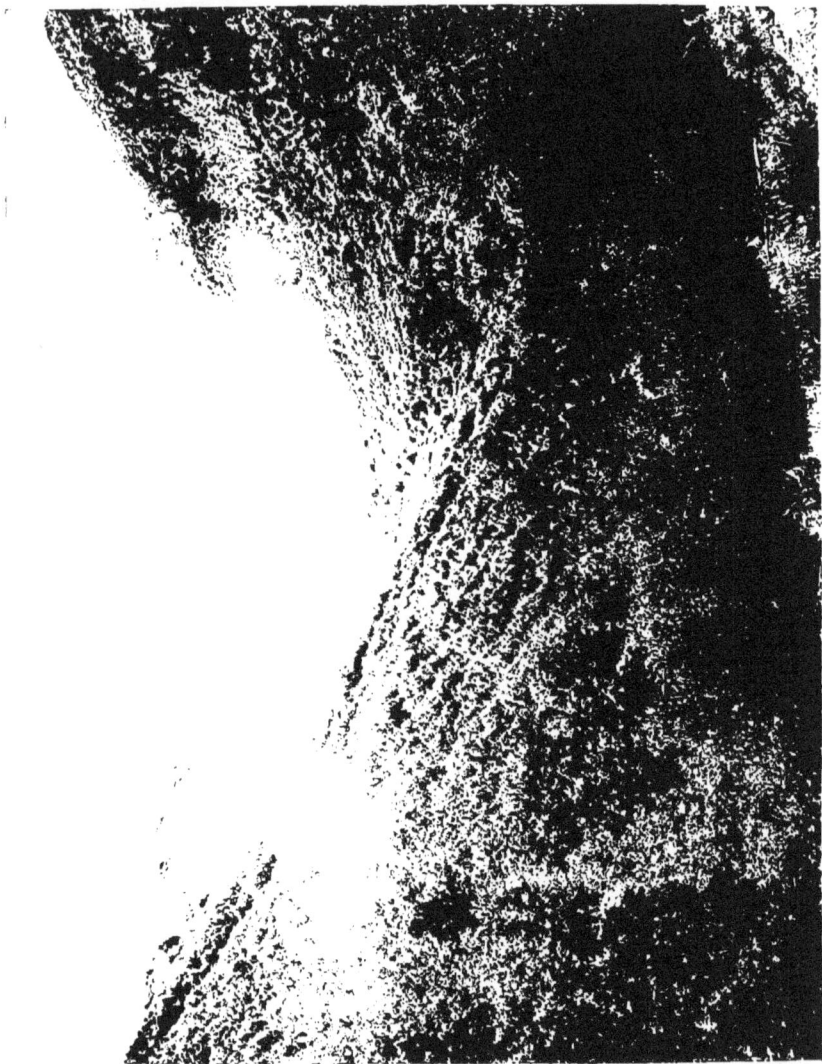

Great Bear Canyon from the Western Slope of Mount Markham.

FROM ORANGE GROVES AND ROSES TO SNOW, on the Line of the Mount Lowe Railway.

It was a glorious March morning in the Year of Grace 1893 when the accompanying party of ladies and gentlemen met in one of the flower embowered spots of the San Gabriel Valley. The ladies wore costumes, which, in their light airiness, suggested midsummer. The day was like most of the Spring days in Pasadena, with flowers in endless variety blooming on every hand. Humming-birds in restless activity were darting to and fro, sipping the hidden sweets of the flowers. The mocking birds were imitating the sweet songs of the lark and thrush. The heavens bent smilingly down, and the breezes were soft and balmy. No spring scene in fair Normandy could have been more perfect than the one they gazed upon. They plucked roses of many kinds, enjoyed the arbor of delicate heliotrope which never ceases blooming, and reveled in odors, sights and sounds generally attributed only to " Araby the Blest " or the Vale of Cashmere.

The gentlemen then pointed to the Sierra Madre mountains and informed their companions that they were about to make a trip up to the snow. The ladies, familiar with snow in the East, laughed at the idea of their cavaliers being in snow-drifts within an hour's time, and one of them, pointing to the sunshine, birds, flowers, humming birds and butterflies, was a perfect "doubting Thomas" and laughed at the idea.

Knowing well, however, what was before them, the gentlemen started for the mountains with an outfit including plenty of wraps, overcoats, and other comforts, and yet, even to them it did not seem possible that snow of such depth to any extent could be so near.

At the time of their trip the electric cars were not running from Altadena Junction so they rode horseback, the photographer accompanying them in order to preserve a pictorial record of their adventures.

Reaching Rubio Canyon they took their seats in the construction cars of the Great Cable Incline, and, as they ascended, they gazed upon the rich panorama of the San Gabriel Valley, resplendent in the fresh glory of its Spring robes, when, suddenly, as they were projected over the "buckle" from the 58 per cent. to the 48 per cent. grade of the Incline, they found themselves in a realm of clouds, snow and vapor. Clouds before, clouds behind,—clouds above,—clouds below, clouds all around. For sometime they watched the changing cloud-scenes. Like a well disciplined army the vaporous masses seemed to be ever marshalling themselves afresh, and just as the camera was in position, they opened, and revealed to the entranced spectators a portion of the valley below bathed in sweetest sunshine.

After partaking of refreshments on Echo Mountain, where several inches of snow had fallen, they rode up Castle Canyon, the snow getting deeper as they ascended, until they crossed over the Mount Lowe Saddle, and stood at the head of Grand Canyon. The accom-

From Orange Groves and Roses to Snow.　Among the Flowers in sight of Snow.

panying engravings give but a faint comprehension of the glorious scene presented to them. To the left, pines, firs, balsams, sycamores, maples, oaks and other trees were laden with snow, and stood silent, solemn, awe-inspiring.

On the other side the scene was enlivened by the presence of the party riding forward on the grade of the railroad, which here begins to wind around the slopes of Mount Lowe.

Reaching Crystal Springs, tired though they were, they improvised a toboggan, and dashed for several hundred yards down a natural toboggan slide, until a line of immense pines debarred further progress.

After indulging in other winter sports they retired to rest in the log-cabin of the workmen. But when they arose on the morning of March 9, the snow had fallen so vigorously, though silently, that the cabin was half buried, and all eyes were compelled to engage in a search for the bridle-road upon which they had ridden but a few hours before.

The trees were now heavily laden, and stood, with bowed branches, silent as soldiers with grounded arms. The party felt, however, that an attempt must be made to reach the summit of Mount Lowe, so, once again on their mules, they plodded forward. Here and there the over-hanging trees had sheltered the bridle-road, but everywhere else it was buried deep, and traveling became more difficult.

Jason Brown - the son of the hero of Harper's Ferry, and who was then employed by Professor Lowe on Echo Mountain strode manfully on, until, at last, the advance guard of the party came to a number of trees, which the weight of the snow had so bent over as to render further progress impossible, unless a way was cut through with axes.

As they had none of these weapons, they held a consultation.

The mules unanimously counselled retreat, the Kansas hero was for going forward, the rest knew not what to do, and so, there, far above the clouds, debating as to whether they should proceed or return,—"Snow-bound in the Sierra Madre Switzerland,"—we, for the time being, leave them.

It must not be imagined, however, from this brief sketch, that deep snow often falls on the Sierra Madre Mountains. Two or three times in a year, perhaps, it may thus fall, but such are the peculiar climatic conditions, that on the North side of the range the snow will remain for from four to six weeks after but one fall.

Therefore, it is reasonable to suppose, that now the Mount Lowe Railway is in daily operation to the summit of Echo Mountain, the Company will be enabled to offer to its patrons during the winter months many opportunities to take the delightful and novel ride "From Orange Groves and Roses to Snow."

The Last Bridge of the Great Cable Incline on Summit of Echo Mountain. Looking Through the Clouds Upon the Valley.

From Orange Groves and Roses to Snow.

"From Orange Groves and Roses to Snow."   Tobogganing on the Side of Mount Lowe, at Crystal Springs.

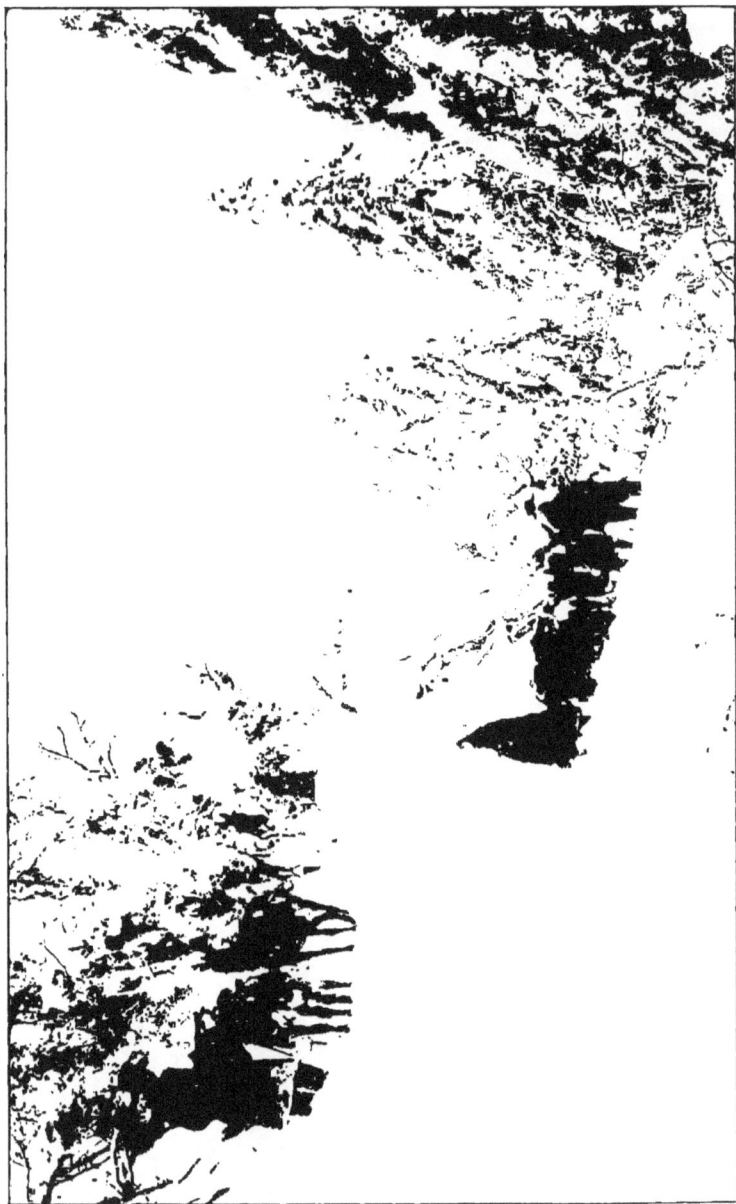

"From Orange Groves and Roses to Snow." "Snow Bound" on the Side of Mount Lowe, March 9, 1893, 6000 Feet above the Sea.

www.ingramcontent.com/pod-product-compliance
Lightning Source LLC
Chambersburg PA
CBHW021434090426
42739CB00009B/1473